The Glass Door

An Adaptation of
Hedda Gabler
by Henrik Ibsen

Adapted by Stephen Evans

"The life of reality isn't livable."

Henrik Ibsen
Notes on Hedda Gabler

ISBN: 9781953725424

 Time Being Media LLC

Contents

Contents v

About the Adaptation............................. vii

Source xi

The Set.. xiii

Musical Notes xv

Direction.. xvii

Cast of Characters...................................... xix

Act I...1

Act Two 45

Act Three..73

About Stephen Evans 99

Books by Stephen Evans 101

About the Adaptation

Several years ago, I was asked by a friend to do an adaptation of *Hedda Gabler* by Henrik Ibsen, which he wanted to direct at a local theater. I did a quick adaptation in my usual fashion: cutting the first act entirely, and making small changes throughout the rest of the play. I sent it to him, and we probably both forgot about it.

My father was very proud of his Norwegian ancestry. His great grandparents on both sides emigrated to the US and settled in the Midwest sometime in the mid Nineteenth century. So Ibsen had some resonance for me. When I came across my initial version of Hedda again last year, I decided to do a more thorough job of it.

Hedda Gabler is still a popular play, with productions around the world each year. For Ibsen, its popularity is second only to *A Doll's House.*

Hedda, like *Hamlet*, is a potboiler of a drama built around a single unique and fascinating character. I imagine a lot of the initial interest in

Hedda was because audiences had never seen anything like her before. The problem with plays built around something new is that they don't stay new. Though perhaps *Hamlet* is an exception to that, as Shakespeare is an exception to most rules.

In this adaptation, I had no intention of either being faithful to Ibsen, or not being faithful. I have tried to change the aspects of the play that I felt would make it the best experience for an audience today.

So, for example, I rewrote the mannered dialogue (which perhaps may be due more to translation than Ibsen) that doesn't sound right to the modern (or at least my) ear. I have also used the character's personal names instead of Mr. This and Mrs. That.

In addition, I have tried to make Hedda's character more coherent, at least to me. Possibly this is a mistake, but I couldn't help myself.

I also had it in mind to enable a production to be set in the present day. One of the difficult issues with this is that a central action revolves around the destruction of a manuscript[1]. In Ibsen's time, it is conceivable that there might be only one copy. Today that is hard to believe. But I have done my

---

[1] A conundrum I also faced in my play *The Ghost Writer*.

best to make it so, and kept Ibsen's device of the manuscript and the stove.

The biggest change of course is that I have cut Ibsen's first act. I tried this first with my adaptation of *As You Like It* many years ago. Again, this is in keeping with the expectations of modern audiences, which are used to greater ambiguity in productions (and every other aspect of life I suppose).

In the end, I like this adaptation better than the original.

I doubt Ibsen would say the same.

Stephen Evans

Source

The primary source for this adaptation of *Hedda Gabler* is an early translation by Edmund Gosse and William Archer, courtesy of The Project Guttenberg Foundation[2]. I have also consulted the original Norwegian text supplied by the Bibliotheca Polyglotta[3] of the University of Oslo.

Ibsen, though he lived most of the time in Italy and Germany, wrote in the Dano-Norwegian language Rigsmål that was the primary language of both Denmark and Norway at the time. This language is somewhat different from the Bokmål version I have learned, which is current in Norway today. But if I need to order pizza in Bergen, I am in good shape.

---

[2] https://www.gutenberg.org/about/pglaf.html
[3] https://www2.hf.uio.no/polyglotta/

STEPHEN EVANS

The Set

This is Ibsen's description:

A spacious, handsome, and tastefully furnished drawing room, decorated in dark colours. In the back, a wide doorway with curtains drawn back, leading into a smaller room decorated in the same style as the drawing-room. In the right-hand wall of the front room, a folding door leading out to the hall. In the opposite wall, on the left, a glass door, also with curtains drawn back. Through the panes can be seen part of a verandah outside, and trees covered with autumn foliage. An oval table, with a cover on it, and surrounded by chairs, stands forward. In front, by the wall on the right, a wide stove of dark porcelain, a high-backed arm-chair, a cushioned foot-rest, and two footstools. A settee, with a small round table in front of it, fills the upper right-hand corner. In front, on the left, a little way from the wall, a sofa. Further back than the glass door, a piano. On either side of the doorway at the back a whatnot with terra-cotta and majolica ornaments. Against the back wall of the inner room a sofa, with a table, and one or two chairs. Over the sofa hangs the portrait of a handsome elderly man in a General's uniform. Over the table a hanging lamp, with an opal glass shade. A number of bouquets are arranged about the drawing-room, in vases and glasses. Others lie upon the tables. The floors in both rooms are covered with thick carpets. - Morning light. The sun shines in through the glass door.

This set is complicated and would be difficult to produce in small theaters, or theaters in the round, or small theaters in the round.

So I imagined a simpler unit set:

- One room.

- A sofa big enough for three.

- Several chairs.

- A desk.

- A piano.

- A wood stove.

As for exits, there are:

- A hallway door that leads to the front door to the house.

- Another door that leads to the interior.

- And of course, the glass door that leads to the garden.

Musical Notes

In the original version, the piano is onstage in Act I, then moved offstage for the final three acts (Hedda comments that it doesn't go with her new things). Hedda plays a few chords in the first act. In Act IV, we have this exchange:

> *HEDDA goes into the back room and draws the curtains. A short pause. Suddenly she is heard playing a wild dance on the piano.*

MRS. ELVSTED.
[Starts from her chair.]
Oh--what is that?

TESMAN.
[Runs to the doorway.]
Why, my dearest Hedda--don't play dance-music to-night! Just think of Aunt Rina! And of Eilert too!

HEDDA.
[Puts her head out between the curtains.]
And of Aunt Julia. And of all the rest of them. After this, I will be quiet.

[Closes the curtains again.]

I have cut this exchange, finding it a bit over the top for my taste. But I like the allusion of Hedda as a merciless Bacchae (and Lovborg as Pentheus). So I kept the piano onstage, both because it is visually interesting and I think Hedda should play it from time to time, providing the score for the play I imagine is always going on in her head.

Direction

This is not a play that holds together very well if you give the audience time to think. So keep the pace moving.

Ibsen also had very specific ideas about set design and who does what where. I left in only the most critical stage direction, everything else being the director's job in my view. And because as a playwright, I have very limited visual sense (which is why my plays consist almost exclusively of dialogue). I rely on the director and actor's to give them shape.

Speaking of which, I also eliminated most of the parenthetic direction Ibsen seemed to enjoy. I prefer to let the actors decide how the words should be read. This is the actor's job, and to some extent the director's, not the playwright's.

I am guessing the runtime of this adaptation is about 80 minutes.

Estimated Times:

Act I: 40 minutes.

Act II: 20 minutes.

Act III: 20 minutes.

Two fifteen-minute intermissions would make the run time under two hours, maybe a half-hour shorter than the original.

Cast of Characters

HEDDA	Formerly Hedda Gabler, now Married to George Tesman.
BRACK	A family friend.
GEORGE	A historian.
Berta	Housekeeper.
ERIC	A family friend.
THEA	An old friend of Hedda's.
AUNT JULIA	George's aunt.

Scene: A villa.

Time: Whenever

STEPHEN EVANS

Act I

Setting: A room at the Tesman's Villa. There is a sofa, several chairs, a desk, a piano, and a wood stove. There is a hallway door, another door, and a glass door that leads to the garden.

At Rise: Hedda is alone in the room. She stands by the open glass door loading a pistol. The other of the pair lies in an open case on the writing-table.

She points through the glass door and fires. She raises the pistol again and fires. And again.

Judge Brack appears in the hallway door.

BRACK
Are you mad!

HEDDA
No. I'm bored.

He crosses to her, peers out through the glass

door.

BRACK
What are you shooting at?

HEDDA
Nothing.

*Brack shuts the glass door and gently takes
the pistol out of her hand.*

BRACK
Ah—I gave this set of pistols to your father.

HEDDA
He taught me to shoot.

BRACK
He should have taught you when not to. Where's
the case?

Hedda points.

*He pulls out the other pistol, weighs them
both in his hands, then lays them in the case,
shuts it, and places it on the desk.*

BRACK
Let's not play that game anymore today.

HEDDA
What else is there to do?

BRACK

Is your husband at home? I have invited him to
join me tonight.

*Hedda moves to the desk and puts the pistol-
case in a drawer which she shuts.*

HEDDA

He is not here.

BRACK

Then I should have come a little—earlier.

Hedda crosses the room.

HEDDA

Then I would have been dressing.

BRACK

Exactly.

HEDDA

My husband is not likely to be back for some
time.

BRACK

I'm not impatient.

*Hedda seats herself in the corner of the sofa.
Brack lays his overcoat over the back of the
nearest chair and sits. A short silence. They
look at each other.*

HEDDA

Well?

>   BRACK
Well?

>   HEDDA
I asked first.

>   *Brack bends a little forward.*

>   BRACK
Come, let's be cozy, Mrs. Hedda.

>   *Hedda leans back.*

>   HEDDA
Seems like an eternity since our last talk, Judge
Brack.

>   BRACK
One to one you mean.

>   HEDDA
Since you put it so.

>   BRACK
Not a day passed while you were away that I did
not wish you home again.

>   HEDDA
Me too.

>   BRACK
Really? You didn't enjoy your honeymoon?

>   HEDDA
More or less.

BRACK

Your husband has spoken of nothing but happiness.

HEDDA

Nothing makes him happier than grubbing in libraries and making copies of old parchments, or whatever he does. Six months of it. Imagine!

BRACK

Well, that is his vocation in life—or part of it at any rate.

HEDDA

How mortally bored I have been.

BRACK

Really?

HEDDA

Six whole months—interminably in the company of one and the same person.

BRACK

Morning, noon, and night, yes—at all possible times and seasons.

HEDDA

I said 'interminably'.

BRACK.

You seem in splendid condition. Filled out, even. Perhaps the mountain air.

HEDDA.
I am exactly as I was when I started. And George is—a scholar.

BRACK
Undeniable.

HEDDA
And scholars are not at all amusing to travel with. Not in the long run at any rate.

BRACK
Not even—the scholar one happens to love?

HEDDA
Don't use that ridiculous word!

BRACK
I see.

HEDDA
To hear of nothing but the history of civilization, morning, noon, and night—

BRACK
Interminably. But then, why?

HEDDA
My marriage to George?

BRACK
For lack of a better term.

HEDDA
I was bored. And he was determined. So I thought: why not?

BRACK

In that light.

Hedda looks at him sharply.

HEDDA

It was more than my other admirers were
prepared to do for me.

Brack laughs.

HEDDA

I didn't mean to you.

BRACK

Well, I can't answer for all the rest; but as for
myself, I have always entertained a—a certain
respect for the marriage tie—for marriage as an
institution. All I require is a pleasant and intimate
space, where I can make myself useful and am
free to come and go as—as a trusted friend. Such
a triangular friendship—if I may call it so—is very
convenient for all parties.

HEDDA

I longed for a third on our travels.

BRACK

Fortunately your nuptial journey is over now.

HEDDA

I have only arrived at the next station.

BRACK

Well, then the passengers should jump up and move about a little.

HEDDA

No.

BRACK

Really?

HEDDA

No—because there is always someone standing by to—

BRACK

To stare?

HEDDA

Precisely.

BRACK

But—

HEDDA

It always ends in public humiliation. I cannot imagine anything worse.

BRACK

But suppose a third person were to jump in and join the couple.

HEDDA

Ah—that's different.

BRACK

A trusted, sympathetic friend—

HEDDA
—with conversation on all sorts of lively topics—

BRACK
—and not the least bit of a scholar!

HEDDA
That would be a relief.

A door opens offstage. Brack glances in that direction.

HEDDA
And the journey continues.

George enters from the hall with books under his arm and in his pockets.

GEORGE
What a load for a warm day—all these books. I'm positively perspiring, Hedda.

He crosses to the desk and lays them down.

GEORGE
Are you here already, Judge?

Brack stands.

BRACK
I could not wait.

HEDDA
What books have you got there?

GEORGE
New books in my field.

HEDDA
Your field?

BRACK
Yes, books in his field.

Brack and Hedda exchange a confidential smile.

HEDDA
Don't you have enough books in your field?

GEORGE
I must keep up.

HEDDA
I suppose.

GEORGE
And look here—

Searching among his books.

GEORGE
I have got hold of Eric Lovborg's new book too.

He offers it to her. She shakes her head. He puts it back in the pile.

BRACK
Lovborg has written a book? Astonishing. When I knew him. Well, I'm surprised he could write at all. What do you think of it—as a scholar?

GEORGE
I have only skimmed it. But it seems...remarkable.
He never wrote like that when we were in school
together.

He puts the books together.

GEORGE
I'll take these to my study. And then I have to
change for our evening, Judge.

BRACK
No hurry.

GEORGE
By-the-way, Hedda—Aunt Julia is not coming this
evening.

HEDDA
I must bear my disappointment. Was it the hat?

GEORGE
Aunt Rina is very ill.

HEDDA
She always is.

GEORGE
Worse than usual today, poor dear.

Hedda moves to the glass door, stares out.

HEDDA
Worse. Than usual.

George exits.

BRACK

What hat?

HEDDA

A little episode with George's Aunt Julia this morning. She put her hat on the chair and I pretended to think it was our housekeeper's.

BRACK

Hedda!

She shrugs, moves back into the room.

HEDDA

Sometimes I can't resist.

She throws herself down in the easy chair. Brack moves behind her.

BRACK

You're not happy.

HEDDA

I know of no reason why I should be—happy. Can you give me one?

BRACK

This place. You had your heart set on this house, according to George.

HEDDA

Ha! Don't tell me you believe that myth?

She sighs, continuing to stare out the glass door.

HEDDA

One night last summer I made George see me home.

BRACK

I, unfortunately, had to go a different way.

HEDDA

That's true. You were going a different way last summer.

Brack laughs.

HEDDA

We happened to pass here one evening; George was writhing in the agony over having to make conversation; so I took pity—

BRACK

You took pity?

HEDDA

I happened to say, making conversation, that I like this villa. So day after day we kept on talking about it, because we could find nothing else to say. And from that came engagement, marriage, our wedding, the honeymoon, and all the interminable rest of it.

BRACK

Pity has consequences. That is why I never indulge.

HEDDA

Very wise, I'm sure.

BRACK
And you never really cared for the house?

HEDDA
The rooms all smell of lavender and dried rose-leaves. It reminds me of a bouquet the day after a funeral. I'm so bored here.

BRACK
You need a job.

HEDDA
A job?

BRACK
Possibly.

HEDDA
Can you imagine? I often wonder whether I might not get George to go into politics.

Brack laughs.

BRACK
George? Not his line.

HEDDA
No. But if I could get him into it all the same?

BRACK
Why would you want to push him into it?

HEDDA
Because I'm bored!

BRACK
To get into politics, he would have to be rich.

Hedda moves away from the door, sits.

HEDDA
This genteel poverty makes life pitiful. And
boring.

BRACK
The fault may lie elsewhere.

HEDDA
Where?

BRACK
You need a challenge.

HEDDA
A challenge?

BRACK
And now you may perhaps have one in store.

*Hedda gives him a dark stare. Brack looks
back innocently.*

HEDDA
Oh. You mean this ridiculous appointment to the
University?

BRACK
What else?

HEDDA

Eric Lovborg of all people has returned. He has somehow managed to get his life together and write a book. And now he will compete for the teaching position promised to my husband. Or so I heard from Thea.

BRACK

Aha—Senator Elvsted's wife is in town? Last I heard Eric was living up near them.

HEDDA

The Eric I knew was a lecherous drunk.

BRACK

One that you took an interest in.

HEDDA

Jealous?

They laugh, without humor.

HEDDA

Apparently Thea has managed to reform him. But she is terribly worried that this city will tempt him back into his old ways.

BRACK

And will you help him with that?

HEDDA

That is George's problem, not mine.

BRACK

But suppose that an 'obligation' arose?

HEDDA
No 'obligations' for me!

BRACK
As a mother, you would control a human destiny?
Surely that would be interesting.

She moves back to the glass door.

HEDDA
There is only one thing in the world I have any
aptitude for.

He moves to her.
BRACK
What?

She turns to him.

HEDDA
Boring myself to death.

She laughs.

HEDDA
Here comes the Professor, right on cue.

George enters, dressed for the party.

GEORGE
Hedda, have you heard from Eric? I invited him
here.

HEDDA
No, George.

GEORGE
He'll be here.

BRACK
Do you really think he will come?

GEORGE
Of course. Oh. You have heard that rumor about his competing for the professorship. Nonsense.

BRACK
You think so?

GEORGE
Eric is an old friend. He would never stand in my way.

BRACK
Well then, that's settled.

Brack stands, picks up his coat.

GEORGE
I should wait for him as long as possible.

He puts his coat back on the chair and sits again.

BRACK
None of my guests will arrive before seven. We have time yet.

George turns to Hedda.

GEORGE
Then we can keep Hedda company!

HEDDA

How wonderful.

Hedda pauses, thinking.

HEDDA

At worst, Eric can stay with me.

BRACK

What do you mean by 'At worst'?

HEDDA

If he won't go with you and George. Thea is coming. We three can have tea together.

GEORGE

Oh yes. Fine.

BRACK

And that would perhaps be the safest plan for him.

HEDDA

Why so?

BRACK

In view of his—former proclivities?

HEDDA

Eric's a converted sinner.

Berta appears at the hall door.

BERTA

There's a gentleman asking if you are at home, ma'am.

HEDDA
Well, show him in.

Eric enters from the hall. He is slim and lean; of the same age as George, but looks older and somewhat worn-out. He stops near the door, seeming somewhat embarrassed. George goes up to him and shakes his hand warmly.

GEORGE
Eric. Good to see you again. It has been—

ERIC
Thank you for your invitation, George.

HEDDA
I am glad to see you, Eric. I don't know whether you two gentlemen—?

ERIC
Judge Brack.

BRACK
Oh yes—in the old days we were well acquainted.

GEORGE
And now Eric you must make yourself entirely at home. I hear you are going to settle in town again.

ERIC
Yes, I am.

GEORGE

About time. I have your new book, but I haven't had time to read it yet.

ERIC

Don't bother.

GEORGE

Why?

ERIC

Because there is little in it to bother about.

GEORGE

Why do you say that? It has received excellent reviews, I hear.

ERIC

That was what I wanted; so I put nothing into the book except what everyone would agree with.

BRACK

Very wise of you.

GEORGE

But Eric!

ERIC

Now I mean to win myself a position again.

GEORGE

Ah, I see.

Eric draws a packet wrapped in paper from his coat pocket.

ERIC

For this is the real book—the book I have put my true self into.

GEORGE

What's it about?

ERIC

The future. There are two sections. The first deals with an analysis of cultural forces. And the second—forecasting the probable course of human civilization.

GEORGE

I would never have thought of writing anything of that sort.

Hedda is back at the glass door, drumming on the pane.

HEDDA

Who would?

Eric opens the packet. It is a manuscript.

GEORGE

It's hand-written.

ERIC

I will have to have it transcribed one of these days, but I keep making changes. And Thea, Mrs. Elvsted, can't type. She was my amanuensis.

HEDDA

Was she?

Eric replaces the manuscript in its paper and lays the packet on the table.

ERIC
I thought I might read a little of it to you this evening.

Brack looks at Hedda, then back to Eric.

BRACK
Eric—there is a little gathering at my house this evening—in honor of George. I hope you will join us.

ERIC
No, I can't—thank you very much.

BRACK
A select circle. And I we shall have a "lively time," as Mrs. Hedda says.

ERIC
No doubt. But—

BRACK
You could bring your manuscript with you. I'm very interested in the future.

GEORGE
Why not?

HEDDA
I am sure Eric would prefer to remain here and have supper.

ERIC

With you?

HEDDA

And with Thea.

ERIC

Oh.

HEDDA

So you see you must stay, Eric, so you can see her safely home. In this city, one never knows what can happen.

ERIC

In that case I will stay.

Hedda goes to the hall door. Berta enters. Hedda talks to her in a whisper. Berta nods and goes out again.

GEORGE

They told me you were planning a lecture series this autumn.

ERIC

I hope you don't mind.

GEORGE

No! Of course not.

ERIC

You are worried it might impact your chances of an appointment to the university.

GEORGE

Oh, I can't expect you, out of consideration for me, to—

ERIC

But I plan to wait till after you have received your appointment.

GEORGE

Are you not going to compete for the position?

ERIC

No.

GEORGE

Hedda! Eric is not going to stand in our way!

HEDDA

Leave me out of it.

GEORGE

You see Eric, Hedda and I married on the strength of those prospects.

HEDDA

A prospective marriage.

BRACK

The thunderstorm has passed over.

HEDDA

A drink, gentlemen?

BRACK

Sure.

GEORGE
Just the thing!

HEDDA
Will you not join them, Eric?

ERIC
Nothing for me.

BRACK
It's not poison.

ERIC
Perhaps not for everyone.

HEDDA
I will keep Eric company in the meantime.

GEORGE
Yes, yes, Hedda dear, do.

*George and Brack exit. Eric remains
standing. Hedda goes to the desk.*

HEDDA
Raising her voice a little.
Do you care to look at some photographs, Eric?
You know George and I toured the Tyrol on our
way home.

*She takes up an album and moves to the sofa.
Eric approaches, stops, and looks at her.
Then he seats himself to her left. Hedda
opens the album.*

HEDDA

Do you see this range of mountains, Eric? It's the
Ortler group. George has written the name
underneath. Here it is: "The Ortler group near
Meran."

ERIC

Hedda Gabler.

HEDDA

Hush!

ERIC

Softly.
Hedda Gabler!

HEDDA

Looking at the album.
That was my name.

ERIC

And I must teach myself never to say Hedda
Gabler again.

HEDDA

Still turning over the pages.
The sooner the better.

ERIC

Hedda Gabler married to—George Tesman.

HEDDA

Interminably.

ERIC

Married to George.

George comes into the room with a drink and goes towards the sofa.

HEDDA

Just look at these peaks! What's the name of these curious peaks, dear?

GEORGE

Let me see. Oh, those are the Dolomites.

HEDDA

Those are the Dolomites, Eric.

GEORGE

Hedda, dear, would you like a drink?

HEDDA

Yes, please; and perhaps a few hors d'oevre.

George exits. He passes Brack, who keeps an eye on Hedda and Eric from the doorway.

ERIC

Do you love George?

Hedda laughs.

HEDDA

What a concept!

George enters with a small tray from the inner room.

GEORGE

Here you are!

He puts the tray on the table.

HEDDA

Two glasses? Eric said he wouldn't have any—

GEORGE

No, but Thea will soon be here, won't she?

HEDDA

Yes, Thea.

Shows him a picture.
Do you remember this little village?

GEORGE

Just below the Brenner Pass. We spent the night
there.

HEDDA

And those tourists.

GEORGE

Yes. Imagine—if we could only have had you
with us, Eric! Eh?

He exits.

ERIC

Answer me one thing, Hedda—

HEDDA

Well?

ERIC

Was there no love in your friendship for me?

HEDDA

I remember—two intimate friends. There was something beautiful, fascinating, daring.

ERIC

I would come to your father's house in the afternoon—and the General sat over at the window reading his papers—with his back towards us—

HEDDA

And we two on the corner sofa—

ERIC

Always with the same magazine in front of us—

HEDDA

For want of an album, yes.

ERIC

I told you about myself, things that at that time no one else knew. What power in you forced me to confess?

HEDDA

Power? In me?

ERIC

And all those roundabout questions.

HEDDA

Which you understood so well.

ERIC

Your questions were so—frank.

HEDDA
I thought they were roundabout.

ERIC
Yes, but frank nevertheless, about—everything.

HEDDA
A girl's curiosity.

ERIC
So that was all it was? Curiosity?

HEDDA
Partly. And also companionship.

ERIC
In the hunger for life. But why couldn't it
continue?

HEDDA
You.

ERIC
It was you that broke off with me.

HEDDA
Yes, when our friendship threatened to develop
into something more serious. We were—true
companions.

ERIC
You threatened to shoot me.

HEDDA
It's a bad habit.

ERIC
Why didn't you?

HEDDA
I had my reputation to think of.

ERIC
You are a coward at heart.

HEDDA
A terrible coward. Lucky for you. And now you have found consolation at the Elvsteds.

ERIC
I know what Thea has confided to you.

HEDDA
And perhaps you have confided to her something about us?

ERIC
Not a word. She is too foolish to understand.

HEDDA
Foolish?

ERIC
About such matters.

HEDDA
And I am cowardly. But now I'll confess something to you.

ERIC
Well?

HEDDA
The fact that I did not shoot you —

ERIC
Yes!

HEDDA
That was not my cowardice—that evening.

Twilight has begun to fall. Berta opens the hall door. Thea appears.

HEDDA
Thea! We were just wondering about you.

Thea enters from the hall.

HEDDA
My sweet Thea!

Thea gives Hedda her hand. Eric has risen. He and Thea greet each other with a silent nod.

THEA
Your husband?

HEDDA
He and Judge Brack will be going soon.

THEA
Are they going out?

HEDDA
Yes, to a party.

THEA
To Eric
Not you?

HEDDA
Eric will remain with us.

Thea takes a chair and is about to seat herself at his side.

HEDDA
Thea! Not there! Come here. I will sit between you.

THEA
As you please.

She sits on the sofa on Hedda's right. Eric re-seats himself on Hedda's left.

ERIC
Isn't she lovely to look at?

HEDDA
Only to look at?

ERIC
Thea and I are true companions. We have absolute faith in each other; so we can sit and talk with perfect frankness.

HEDDA
Not roundabout, Eric?

THEA
He says I have inspired him.

HEDDA

I'm sure you have.

ERIC

She is so brave, Hedda!

THEA

Am I brave?

ERIC

Where your companion is concerned.

HEDDA

If only!

ERIC

What do you mean?

HEDDA

Then life would be livable. Thea, you really must have a drink.

THEA

No, thank you.

HEDDA

Well then, you, Eric.

ERIC

No, thank you.

THEA

No, he doesn't either. For the last two years.

HEDDA

But if I insist?

ERIC
It would be of no use.

HEDDA
Then I have no power over you?

ERIC
Not in that respect.

HEDDA
But. Eric. I think you ought to—for your own sake.

THEA
Why, Hedda?

ERIC
How so?

HEDDA
On account of other people.

ERIC
Indeed?

HEDDA
Other people might think that you did not feel secure. In yourself.

THEA
Oh please, Hedda—!

ERIC
People may suspect what they like.

THEA
Yes, let them!

HEDDA

I saw it plainly in Judge Brack's face a moment ago.

ERIC

What did you see?

HEDDA

His contemptuous smile, when you didn't dare to go with them.

ERIC

Dare? I simply preferred to stay here.

THEA

What could be more natural, Hedda?

HEDDA

But the Judge could not guess that.

ERIC

Whatever.

HEDDA

Then you are not going with them?

ERIC

I will stay here with you and Thea.

THEA

Yes.

HEDDA

Firm as a rock! What did I tell you, Thea. You had no need to worry.

ERIC

Worry?

THEA

Hedda!

HEDDA

You haven't the slightest reason to be in such mortal terror that he will backslide into—

ERIC

Terror?

THEA

Hedda!

HEDDA

Don't get excited!

ERIC

So she was in mortal terror? For me?

THEA

Oh, Hedda!

ERIC

I am touched by your confidence, Thea.

He picks up the glass.

THEA

Eric!

ERIC

Your health, Thea!

*He empties the glass, puts it down, and takes
the second.*

THEA
Oh, Hedda, Hedda—how could you?

HEDDA
How could I?

ERIC
Here's to your health too, Hedda. Thank you for
the truth.

He empties the glass and is about to re-fill it.

HEDDA
No more. Remember you are going out to supper.

THEA
No, no, no!

HEDDA
Hush!

ERIC
Thea—tell me the truth—

THEA
Yes.

ERIC
A little drunk
Does your husband know that you have come
after me?

THEA
Oh, Hedda.

He pours another, picks up the glass.

ERIC
Here's a glass for the old Senator too!

Hedda puts her hand on his.

HEDDA
No more just now. Remember, you have to read
your manuscript tonight.

He drinks anyway.

ERIC
You shall see—both you, and the others! I am no
coward.

THEA
Oh!

*Brack and George enter. Brack takes and
overcoat.*

BRACK
Well, Mrs. Hedda, our time has come.

HEDDA
So it seems.

ERIC
Mine too, Judge Brack.

BRACK
Well, are you coming after all? I'm delighted.

THEA
Oh, Eric, don't do it!

Eric puts the package of the manuscript in his pocket.

ERIC
Thea, I'll come back and fetch you after. At ten or thereabouts, Hedda? Will that do?

HEDDA
Certainly.

GEORGE
Fine. But you must not expect me so early, Hedda.

HEDDA
Stay as long as you please.

THEA
Well then, Eric—I shall remain here until you come.

ERIC
Please do, Thea.

BRACK

Gentlemen! I hope we shall have a lively time, as a certain fair lady puts it.

HEDDA

Ah, if only the fair lady could be present unseen—!

BRACK

Laughing.
Inadvisable.

GEORGE

Also laughing.
Imagine!

BRACK

Good-bye, ladies.

ERIC

About ten o'clock, then.

Brack, Eric, and George exit by the hall door. Thea rises and wanders restlessly about the room. Hedda closes the curtains over the glass door.

THEA

Hedda—Hedda—what will come of all this?

HEDDA

At ten o'clock—he will be here. I can see him already—with vine-leaves in his hair—flushed and fearless.

THEA

Oh, I hope so.

HEDDA

And then, you'll see.

THEA

You have some secret purpose in this, Hedda!

HEDDA

Not so secret. I am interested to see if controlling a human destiny is interesting.

THEA

Why not your own?

HEDDA

I don't know how to get off the train.

THEA

What? Then why not your husband's?

HEDDA

He's not worth the trouble. But you. Thea, I remember when we were in school together, I threatened to burn your hair off.

Hedda takes hold of Thea.

THEA

Let me go!

Berta enters.

BERTA

Tea is laid in the dining-room, ma'am.

HEDDA

We're coming.

THEA

I'm going home.

HEDDA

Nonsense! At ten o'clock—Eric will be here—
with vine-leaves in his hair.

She drags Thea almost by force and exits.

Blackout.

Act Two

Setting: The same room. Morning.

At Rise: Thea, wrapped in a large
shawl, and with her feet on a
footrest, sits sunk back in the
armchair. Hedda, fully
dressed, lies sleeping on the
sofa.

*Berta slips cautiously in by the hall door. She
has a letter in her hand.*

BERTA
A girl has just brought this letter.

THEA
A letter! Give it to me!

BERTA
It's for Dr. Tesman, ma'am.

THEA
Oh.

BERTA
It was Miss Julia's servant that brought it. I'll lay it
here on the table.

THEA
It must soon be daylight now.

BERTA
It is daylight already, ma'am.

THEA
And no one come back yet—!

BERTA
I guessed how it would be.

THEA
You guessed?

BERTA
Yes, when I saw that a certain person had come back to town—and that he went off with them. We've heard about that gentleman before.

THEA
Don't speak so loudly. You'll wake Mrs. Tesman.

BERTA
Very well.

Berta goes out by the hall door. Hedda wakes.

HEDDA
What's that—?

THEA
Only Berta.

HEDDA
Oh, we're here. Now I remember.

She sits up on the sofa, stretches herself, and rubs her eyes.

HEDDA

What time is it, Thea?

THEA

It's past seven.

HEDDA

When did Tesman come home?

THEA

He hasn't.

HEDDA

No?

Thea rises, moves to the glass door.

THEA

No one has.

Hedda yawns, and says with her hand before her mouth.

THEA

Did you get a little sleep?

HEDDA

Oh yes; I think I slept pretty well. You?

THEA

Not for a moment.

Hedda rises and goes towards her.

HEDDA

There's nothing to be alarmed about. I understand what's happened.

THEA

What?

HEDDA

It just went very late at Judge Brack's—

THEA

But still—

HEDDA

And then, you see, George didn't want to come home in the middle of the night.

THEA

Where can he have gone?

HEDDA

His Aunt Julia's. She has his old room ready for him.

THEA

No, he can't be there. A letter has just come for him from there.

Hedda picks up the letter and Looks at the address.

HEDDA

Well then, he stayed at Judge Brack's. And as for Eric—he is sitting there still, with vine-leaves in his hair, reading his manuscript.

THEA

Oh, Hedda. You don't believe that.

HEDDA

You really are a little fool, Thea.

THEA

I suppose I am.

HEDDA

And how mortally tired you look.

THEA

Yes, I am mortally tired.

HEDDA

Go to my room and lie down for a little while.

THEA

Oh I couldn't sleep.

HEDDA

I am sure you could.

THEA

I want to know at once when they come.

HEDDA

I'll let you know.

THEA

Promise me, Hedda.

HEDDA

Just go in and have a nap in the meantime.

THEA

I'll try.

She goes off to the inner room.

Hedda goes up to the glass door and draws back the curtains. The broad daylight streams into the room. Then she takes a mirror from the desk, looks at herself in it, and arranges her hair. Next she presses a button.

Berta presently appears at the hall door.

BERTA

Ma'am?

HEDDA

I'm shivering.

BERTA

Yes ma'am.

Berta stops and listens.

BERTA

The front door, ma'am.

HEDDA

Go.

Berta goes out by the hall door.

Hedda kneels on the footrest and lays some more pieces of wood in the stove.

After a short pause, George enters from the

hall.

HEDDA

Good morning.

GEORGE

Hedda! Up so early?

HEDDA

Very early.

GEORGE

I thought you'd be sound asleep!

HEDDA

Not so loud. Thea is resting in my room.

GEORGE

Was she here all night?

HEDDA

Yes, since no one came to fetch her.

GEORGE

Ah, yes.

Hedda closes the door of the stove and rises.

HEDDA

Well, did you enjoy yourselves?

GEORGE

Have you been worried about me?

HEDDA

No. I asked if you enjoyed yourself.

GEORGE
Oh yes, for once, in a way. Eric read to me.

HEDDA
Well?

GEORGE
I believe it is one of the most remarkable books that have ever been written.

HEDDA
I don't care.

GEORGE
When he finished reading—a horrible feeling came over me.

HEDDA
A horrible feeling?

GEORGE
I pitied him. That he—with all his gifts—should be incorrigible after all.

HEDDA
What do you mean?

GEORGE
I mean that he has no self-control.

HEDDA
Did he have vine-leaves in his hair?

GEORGE
Vine-leaves? No. But he made a long, rambling speech in honor of the woman who had inspired him in his work.

HEDDA
Did he name her?

GEORGE
No, but I assume he meant Thea.

HEDDA
Where did you leave him?

GEORGE
On the way to town. He had drunk much more
than was good for him.

HEDDA
It sounds like it.

GEORGE
I fell a little behind the others.

HEDDA
But—?

GEORGE
What do you think I found?

HEDDA
How should I know!

*From his coat pocket, George takes out a
package wrapped in paper.*

GEORGE
I found this. His precious, irreplaceable
manuscript! He lost it, and knew nothing about it.

HEDDA
But why didn't you give it back to him?

GEORGE
In the state he was in—

HEDDA
Did you tell any of the others?

GEORGE
No.

HEDDA
So no one knows that Eric's manuscript is in your possession?

GEORGE
No.

HEDDA
What did you say to him afterwards?

GEORGE
I didn't talk to him again at all; he and two or three of the others disappeared.

HEDDA
They must have taken him home then.

GEORGE
Perhaps. Is there coffee? Then I must take this to him.

Hedda Holds out her hand for the packet.

HEDDA
Let me read it first.

GEORGE

Can you imagine what a state he'll be in when he wakes and can't find the manuscript?

HEDDA

He has copies surely.

GEORGE

He said not.

HEDDA

Could it be written over again?

GEORGE

I doubt it.

HEDDA

Oh, here is a letter for you. It came early this morning.

Hedda hands to him.

GEORGE

It's from Aunt Julia!

He lays the packet on the desk, opens the letter, reads.

GEORGE

Oh, Hedda—she says poor Aunt Rina is dying!

HEDDA

Well, we knew it was coming.

GEORGE

And that if I want to see her again, I have to hurry. Come with me?

HEDDA

No, no don't ask me. I cannot look upon sickness and death.

GEORGE

I hope I won't be too late.

Berta appears at the hall door.

BERTA

Judge Brack is at the door.

GEORGE

I can't see him now.

HEDDA

Ask Judge Brack to come in.

Berta goes out, followed by George.

Hedda goes to the desk and places the package in the bookcase. Brack enters from the hall.

HEDDA

You are an early bird, I must say.

BRACK

Yes, I am! George was in a hurry.

HEDDA

I hear you made a particularly lively night of it,
Judge Brack.

BRACK

I'm still wearing the same clothes, Mrs. Hedda.

HEDDA

You too?

BRACK

As you see.

HEDDA

Well then, sit down, my dear Judge, and tell your
story in comfort.

*She sits to the left of the table. Brack sits
near her, at the long side of the table.*

HEDDA

So?

BRACK

I had special reasons for keeping track of my
guests—last night.

HEDDA

Of Eric especially, perhaps?

BRACK

Frankly, yes.

HEDDA

And?

BRACK
Do you know where he and one or two of the others finished the night, Mrs. Hedda?

HEDDA
Tell me.

BRACK
They put in an appearance at a particularly animated soiree.

HEDDA
Tell me more.

BRACK
Eric had declined the invitation initially.

HEDDA
I hear he found inspiration.

BRACK
Powerful inspiration. To make a long story short—he landed at last in Madame Diana's rooms.

HEDDA
Madame Diana's?

BRACK
A party, for a select circle of her admirers and her lady friends.

HEDDA
Is she a red-haired woman?

BRACK
Precisely.

HEDDA
A sort of a—singer?

BRACK
In her off moments. Eric was one of her most
enthusiastic fans—in his glory days.

HEDDA
And how did all this end?

BRACK
Far from amicably, apparently. After a tender
reconciliation, they seem to have come to blows.

HEDDA
Eric and her?

BRACK
Yes. He accused her or her friends of having
robbed him. Caused quite a furor.

HEDDA
And?

BRACK
The police came. He struck one of the policemen
and tore the coat off his back. So they hauled him
down to the station.

HEDDA
How did you hear about this?

BRACK
From the police themselves.

HEDDA
No vine-leaves in his hair?

BRACK
Vine-leaves, Mrs. Hedda?

HEDDA
What's your real reason for tracking Eric's movements so carefully?

BRACK
In the first place, he came straight from my house.

HEDDA
Will that matter?

BRACK
Possibly. And, as a friend of the family, it was my duty to supply you and George with a full account of Eric's—nocturnal exploits.

HEDDA
Why?

BRACK
Because I have a shrewd suspicion that he intends to use you as a sort of blind.

HEDDA
There are plenty of other places where he and Thea could meet.

BRACK
Every respectable house will be closed to him.

HEDDA
And so ought mine to be, you mean?

BRACK

Yes. If not, I should find myself homeless.

HEDDA

So you want to be the one cock in the yard.

BRACK

And for that I will fight—with every weapon in my control.

HEDDA

I see you are a dangerous person.

BRACK

You think so?

HEDDA

I'm beginning to. And I'm exceedingly glad that you have no hold over me.

BRACK

Well well, Mrs. Hedda—perhaps you're right. If I had, who knows what I might be capable of?

HEDDA

That sounds almost like a threat.

BRACK

Oh, not at all! The triangle is best when it's mutually beneficial.

HEDDA

There I agree with you.

BRACK

Well, now I have said all I have to say. Goodbye, Mrs. Hedda.

He goes towards the glass door.

HEDDA
Are you going through the garden?

BRACK
Yes, it's a short cut.

HEDDA
And a back way, too.

BRACK
I have no objection to back ways. They can be stimulating at times.

HEDDA
But you never know when there will be target practice going on.

He looks at her, decides to leave by another door. They exchange nods of farewell. He goes. She watches him, then she goes to the bookcase, takes Eric's package out, and is on the point of looking through its contents.

Berta is heard speaking loudly in the hall. Hedda turns and listens. Then she hastily locks up the package in the drawer, and lays the key on the desk.

Eric tears open the hall door. He looks somewhat confused and irritated.

ERIC

I must come in!

He closes the door, turns, sees Hedda, at once regains his self- control.

HEDDA

Well, Eric, this is rather a late hour to call for Thea.

ERIC

And an early hour to call on you. Pardon me.

HEDDA

How do you know she's still here?

ERIC

They told me at her lodgings that she had been out all night.

HEDDA

How did they say it?

ERIC

I'm not sure what you mean.

HEDDA

Did they seem to think it odd?

ERIC

Oh yes, of course! I'm dragging her down with me! I suppose George is not up yet.

HEDDA

No.

ERIC
When did he come home?

HEDDA
Very late.

ERIC
Did he tell you anything?

HEDDA
Yes, that you had had a very good time at Judge
Brack's.

ERIC
Nothing more?

HEDDA
I don't think so. Though I was so quite sleepy—

Thea enters.

THEA
Ah, Eric! At last!

ERIC
Yes, at last. And too late!

THEA
What is too late?

ERIC
Everything is too late now. It is all over with me.

THEA
Don't say that!

ERIC
When you hear—

THEA

I won't hear anything!

HEDDA

Perhaps you would prefer to talk alone?

ERIC

No, stay. Please.

THEA

I won't hear anything.

ERIC

It's not last night's adventures that I want to talk about.

THEA

What then?

ERIC

I want to say—that can't see each other again.

THEA

What!

HEDDA

I knew it!

ERIC

You can help me anymore, Thea.

THEA

Can't help you! Aren't we going to work together anymore?

ERIC

I won't be doing any more work.

THEA

Then what am I to do?

ERIC

You should go on as if you never knew me.

THEA

I can't!

ERIC

Thea, you have to go home again.

THEA

Where you are, I will be! The book.

HEDDA

What book?

ERIC

My book, and Thea's.

THEA

That's how I feel.

ERIC

Thea—our book will never be published.

HEDDA

Ah.

THEA

Never?

ERIC

Never.

THEA

Eric, what have you done with the manuscript?

HEDDA
Yes, the manuscript.

THEA
Where is it?

ERIC
I destroyed it.

THEA
No!

HEDDA
It sounds improbable.

ERIC
It is true, all the same.

THEA
Oh God—oh God, Hedda— his work!

ERIC
I have destroyed my life. Why shouldn't I
destroy my work?

THEA
And you did this last night?

ERIC
Yes! and scattered the pieces. Let them drift and
then sink—deeper and deeper—just like me,
Thea.

THEA
It's like you killed a child.

ERIC

Just.

THEA

How could you? It was my child too.

HEDDA

Ah, the child.

THEA

It is over then. I'll go, Hedda.

HEDDA

Away?

THEA

I see nothing but darkness ahead.

She goes out by the hall door.

HEDDA

Are you going to see her home, Eric?

ERIC

Would you have people see us together?

HEDDA

Is it so utterly irreparable?

ERIC

My life is over.

HEDDA

But all the same, how could you treat her so heartlessly?

ERIC

Don't say that!

HEDDA
To destroy what gave her life meaning and
purpose! You don't call that heartless?

ERIC
I can you tell the truth, Hedda.

HEDDA
The truth?

ERIC
First promise me—give me your word—that what
I tell you now Thea will never know.

HEDDA
I give you my word.

ERIC
Good. What I said just now was untrue.

HEDDA
About the manuscript?

ERIC
Yes. I haven't destroyed it.

HEDDA
Where is it then?

ERIC
I have destroyed it none the less—utterly
destroyed it, Hedda!

HEDDA
I don't understand.

ERIC

Suppose a man came home to his child's mother
after a night of drunkenness and said: "I took our
child with me and I have lost her. I don't know
who may have their hands on her."

HEDDA

It was only a book.

ERIC

Thea's soul was in that book.

HEDDA

What are you going to do?

ERIC

Make an end—the sooner the better.

HEDDA

Yes, Eric. Do it with beauty.

ERIC

With vine-leaves in my hair, as you used to say in
the old days—?

HEDDA

Now go—and don't come here again.

ERIC

Good-bye, Hedda. And tell George...

He is on the point of going.

HEDDA

Wait!

She goes to the desk, takes out one of the
pistols, and sets the case on the desk. Then
she returns to Eric with one of the pistols.

ERIC
What is this?

HEDDA
Don't you recognize it? It was aimed at you once.

ERIC
You should have pulled the trigger.

HEDDA
Take it.

He does.

HEDDA
No one must see you. Go out this way.

She takes him to the glass door, opens it.

ERIC
Good-bye, Hedda Gabler.

Eric exits.

HEDDA
With beauty, Eric Lovborg. Promise me!

He goes out by the glass door.

Hedda listens for a moment at the door.
Then she goes up to the desk, takes out the

manuscript package.

Next she goes to the stove, opens the door. She hesitates, looks around, then puts the package in and closes the door. Light flares through the window in the door as it burns.

HEDDA

Your child is burning, you curly-headed fool. Your child and Eric Lovborg's. I am burning your child.

Berta appears at the hallway door.

BERTA

Are you still cold, ma'am?

Hedda waves her away, and smiles.

Blackout.

Act Three

Setting: The same room. Evening.

At Rise: The curtains over the glass
                       door are drawn closed.

*Hedda, dressed in black, walks to and fro in
the dark room. Each time she moves by the
piano, she strikes discordant chords.*

*Berta enters, eyes red with weeping. She
watches Hedda for a moment, shivers
suddenly, then exits. Hedda goes up to the
glass door, lifts the curtain a little aside, and
looks out into the darkness.*

*Shortly afterwards, Aunt Julia, dressed in
mourning and veiled, comes in from the hall.
Hedda goes towards her and holds out her
hand.*

HEDDA
I have heard the news already, as you see. George
sent me a note.

AUNT JULIA

Yes, he promised me he would. But nevertheless I thought that to Hedda—here in the house of life—I ought myself to bring the tidings of death. My poor sister has at last found peace.

HEDDA

It was kind of you to come.

AUNT JULIA

Ah, Rina ought not to have left us now. This is not the time for this to be a house of mourning.

HEDDA

She died peacefully, did she not, Aunt Julia?

AUNT JULIA

Oh, her end was so calm, so beautiful. And then she had the happiness of seeing George once more, and telling him good-bye. Has he not come home yet?

HEDDA

No. But won't you sit down?

AUNT JULIA

No thank you, my dear, dear Hedda. I should like to, but I have so much to do.

HEDDA

Can I help you in any way?

AUNT JULIA

Oh, you must not think of it! Hedda Tesman must have no hand in such mournful work. Nor let her thoughts dwell on it either—not at this time.

HEDDA

One is not always mistress of one's thoughts.

AUNT JULIA

Ah yes, it is the way of the world.

George enters by the hall door.

HEDDA

Ah, you have come at last.

GEORGE

Aunt Julia?

AUNT JULIA

I was just going, my dear boy. Well, have you done all you promised?

GEORGE

I have forgotten half of it. I can't think today.

AUNT JULIA

George, you mustn't take it in this way.

GEORGE

How do you mean?

AUNT JULIA

Rejoice that she is at rest.

GEORGE

Oh yes, yes—Aunt Rina.

HEDDA

You will be lonely now, Aunt Julia.

AUNT JULIA

At first, yes. But I'll soon find an occupant for Rina's room.

GEORGE

Who?

AUNT JULIA

Oh, there's always someone in want of nursing, unfortunately.

HEDDA

Would you really take on such a burden again?

AUNT JULIA

A burden! No burden to me.

HEDDA

But a total stranger.

AUNT JULIA

I need to have someone to live for. There may soon be something in this house, too, to keep an old aunt busy.

HEDDA

Oh, don't trouble about anything here.

GEORGE

Yes, just imagine what a time we three might have together, if?

HEDDA

If?

GEORGE

Oh nothing.

AUNT JULIA

I must go home to Rina. And you two will want to talk to each other.

Smiling.

And perhaps Hedda may have something to tell you too, George. Good-bye!

She starts to exit, then turns at the door.

AUNT JULIA

How strange it all is.

GEORGE

Yes, imagine!

Aunt Julia goes out by the hall door.

HEDDA

I almost think your Aunt Rina's death affects you more than it does your Aunt Julia.

GEORGE

Oh, it's not just that. It's Eric.

HEDDA

Is there anything new about him?

GEORGE

I looked in at his rooms this afternoon, intending to tell him the manuscript was in safe hands.

HEDDA

Well, did you find him?

GEORGE

No. He wasn't at home. But afterwards I met
Thea, and she told me that he had been here early
this morning.

HEDDA

Yes, directly after you had gone.

GEORGE

And he said that he had destroyed his
manuscript?

HEDDA

Yes.

GEORGE

He must have been completely out of his mind!
And you thought it best not to give it back to him,
Hedda?

HEDDA

No.

GEORGE

But you told him that we had it?

HEDDA

No. Did you tell Thea?

GEORGE

No, I thought I had better not. But you should
have told him.

HEDDA

I have not got it.

GEORGE

Haven't got it?

HEDDA

I burnt it.

GEORGE

Burnt!

HEDDA

Don't scream so. The servant might hear you.

GEORGE

Why?

HEDDA

I advise you not to speak of it—either to Judge Brack or to anyone else.

GEORGE

What possessed you?

HEDDA

I did it for your sake, George.

GEORGE

For my sake!

HEDDA

This morning, when you told me about what he had read to you—

GEORGE

Yes?

HEDDA

You acknowledged that you envied him his work.

GEORGE
I didn't mean that literally.

HEDDA
I could not bear the idea that anyone should outshine you.

GEORGE
Hedda! Is this true?

HEDDA
Just at this time— no, no; you can ask Aunt Julia. She will tell you, fast enough.

GEORGE
I think I understand, Hedda!

HEDDA
Don't shout so. The servant might hear.

GEORGE
The servant! I'll tell Berta myself.

HEDDA
It is killing me, all this!

GEORGE
What is, Hedda?

HEDDA
All this—absurdity.

GEORGE
Oh, Aunt Julia will be so so happy!

HEDDA
When she hears that I have burnt Eric Lovborg's manuscript—for your sake?

GEORGE
No, of course nobody must know about that. But that you love me so much, Hedda—Aunt Julia must really share my joy in that!

Thea, dressed as in the first Act, enters by the hall door.

THEA
Oh, dear Hedda, forgive my coming again.

HEDDA
What is the matter with you, Thea?

GEORGE
Something about Eric again?

THEA
Yes! I am dreadfully afraid.

GEORGE
Why, Thea?

THEA
Incredible rumors.

GEORGE
I heard also.

HEDDA
What did they say at his boarding-house?

THEA
I did not dare to ask.

GEORGE
We must hope that you misunderstood them, Thea.

THEA
No, no; I am sure it was of him they were talking. And I heard something about the hospital or—

GEORGE
The hospital?

THEA
I went to his lodgings and asked for him there.

HEDDA
Did you?

GEORGE
But you didn't find him?

THEA
No. And the people knew nothing about him. I am sure something terrible must have happened to him.

GEORGE
I should make inquiries.

HEDDA
No, don't mix yourself up in this affair.

Brack enters. He looks grave.

GEORGE

Hello, Judge.

BRACK

Sorry to intrude. It was imperative I should see you this evening.

GEORGE

I see you have heard the news about Aunt Rina.

BRACK

Among other things.

GEORGE

Isn't it sad?

BRACK

Depends on how you look at it.

GEORGE

Has something else happened?

BRACK

Yes.

HEDDA

Anything sad, Judge Brack?

BRACK

That, too, depends on how you look at it, Mrs. Tesman.

THEA

It is something about Eric!

BRACK

What makes you think that, Thea?

GEORGE
Oh, for heaven's sake, tell us!

BRACK
Eric Lovborg is dying.

Thea Shrieks.

GEORGE
Dying!

HEDDA
So soon then.

THEA
And we parted in anger!

HEDDA
Thea—be careful.

THEA
I must go to him.

BRACK
Don't.

THEA
Tell me what has happened to him?

GEORGE
Has he harmed himself?

HEDDA
Yes, I am sure he has.

BRACK
Correct, Mrs. Tesman.

THEA

Oh, how horrible!

GEORGE

Imagine!

HEDDA

Shot himself.

BRACK

Rightly guessed again, Mrs. Tesman.

THEA

When did it happen?

BRACK

This afternoon—between three and four.

GEORGE

Where?

BRACK

I don't know exactly. I only know that he was
found. He had shot himself—in the heart.

THEA

Oh, how terrible!

HEDDA

Was it in the heart?

BRACK

As I said.

HEDDA

Not in the temple?

BRACK
In the heart, Mrs. Tesman.

HEDDA
Well, well—the heart is good, too.

BRACK
How do you mean, Mrs. Tesman?

HEDDA
Oh, nothing—nothing.

GEORGE
And the wound is lethal?

BRACK
He is likely dead by now.

THEA
Oh, Hedda!

GEORGE
But tell me, how have you learnt all this?

BRACK
The police.

HEDDA
A deed worth doing.

GEORGE
Hedda! What are you saying?

HEDDA
I say there is beauty in this.

BRACK
Really, Mrs. Tesman?

THEA

Oh, Hedda, how can you speak of beauty in such an act!

HEDDA

Eric has settled his account with life.

THEA

It was madness.

GEORGE

Despair.

HEDDA

No.

THEA

Yes, yes! Madness! Just as when he destroyed our manuscript.

BRACK

The manuscript? Has he destroyed it?

THEA

Yes, last night.

BRACK

Extraordinary.

GEORGE

To think of Eric dying this way. And not leaving behind him the book that would have made his name famous.

THEA

Oh, if only it could be put together again!

GEORGE
Yes, if only.

THEA
Perhaps it can, George.

GEORGE
What do you mean?

THEA
I have kept all his notes.

HEDDA
What?

GEORGE
You kept them!

THEA
Yes, I have them here.

GEORGE
Let me see!

Thea hands him a bundle of papers.

THEA
But they are in such disorder—all mixed-up.

GEORGE
Maybe if we two put our heads together—

THEA
We could try.

GEORGE
I will dedicate my life to this task.

HEDDA
You, George?

GEORGE
My own work must wait in the meantime.

HEDDA
Perhaps.

GEORGE
Thea, we will give ourselves to it. We owe him
that much.

THEA
I will do the best I can.

GEORGE
Come with me, Thea.

> George and Thea exit. Hedda sits. Presently
> Brack goes up to her.

HEDDA
What freedom in this act.

BRACK
Freedom, Mrs. Hedda?

HEDDA
To know that an act of beauty, of courage, is still
possible in this world.

BRACK
Hedda.

> HEDDA

Eric had the courage to live his life as he chose.
And then he had the will to turn away from it
when he chose.

> BRACK

Fantasy.

> HEDDA

Fantasy? What do you mean?

> BRACK

Eric did not shoot himself—voluntarily.

> HEDDA

Not voluntarily?

> BRACK

No.

> HEDDA

How?

> BRACK

For poor Thea's sake, I improved the facts a little.

> HEDDA

What facts?

> BRACK

First, he is already dead.

> HEDDA

At the hospital?

> BRACK

Yes—without regaining consciousness.

HEDDA

What else?

BRACK

This—the event did not happen at his lodgings.

HEDDA

What difference does that make?

BRACK

Eric was found shot in—in Madame Diana's boudoir.

HEDDA

That is impossible, Judge Brack! He cannot have been there again to-day.

BRACK

He was there this afternoon. He went there, he said, to demand the return of something which they had taken from him. Talked wildly about a lost child.

HEDDA

Ah.

BRACK

I thought probably he meant his manuscript; but now I hear he destroyed that himself. So I suppose it must have been his money.

HEDDA

Yes, no doubt. And he was found there?

BRACK

Yes, there. With a pistol in his breast-pocket. The bullet had lodged in a vital organ.

HEDDA

In the heart?

BRACK

No—in the bowels.

HEDDA

Oh. Everything I touch turns ludicrous.

BRACK

There is one more disagreeable point, Hedda.

HEDDA

What?

BRACK

The pistol he carried.

HEDDA

Well?

BRACK

He must have stolen it.

HEDDA

He did not steal it.

BRACK

Hush!

George and Thea enter.

GEORGE

Hedda, dear, would you mind our sitting at your desk?

HEDDA

Let me clear it first.

GEORGE

Oh, you needn't trouble, Hedda. There is plenty of room.

Hedda takes the pistol case, covers it with sheet music, and sets it on a shelf in the bookcase. George and Thea sit down and proceed with their work.

HEDDA

Well, how goes it with Eric's monument?

THEA

Difficult.

GEORGE

We'll manage.

Hedda goes over to the stove, and seats herself on one of the footstools. Brack stands over her, leaning on the chair.

HEDDA

What did you say about the pistol?

BRACK

That he must have stolen it.

HEDDA

Why stolen it?

BRACK

Because every other explanation ought to be impossible, Hedda.

HEDDA

Really?

BRACK

Eric was here this morning. Was he not?

HEDDA

Yes.

BRACK

Were you alone with him?

HEDDA

Part of the time.

BRACK

Did you leave the room?

HEDDA

No.

BRACK

Try to recollect. Weren't you out of the room for a moment?

HEDDA

Yes, perhaps just a moment—out in the hall.

BRACK

And where was your pistol-case during that time?

HEDDA

I had it locked up in—

BRACK

Well, Mrs. Hedda?

HEDDA

There on the desk.

BRACK

Have you looked since, to see whether both the pistols are there?

HEDDA

No.

BRACK

Well, you needn't. I saw the pistol found in Eric's pocket, and I knew it at once as the one I had seen yesterday.

HEDDA

Do you have you it with you?

BRACK

The police have it.

HEDDA

What will they do with it?

BRACK

Search till they find the owner.

HEDDA

Do you think they will succeed?

BRACK
Bends over her and whispers.
No, Hedda Gabler—not so long as I say nothing.

HEDDA
And if you do not say nothing, what then?

Brack shrugs, smiles.

HEDDA
I'd rather die.

BRACK
People say such things—but they don't do them.

HEDDA
And supposing the pistol's owner is discovered?

BRACK
An inquest.

HEDDA
Inquest?

BRACK
You will, of course, be brought before the court.

HEDDA
But I have nothing to do with this business.

BRACK
You will have to answer the question: Did you
give Eric the gun? Did you know his mental state?
Are you an accessory? Was there a conspiracy?

Hedda sits.

BRACK

Fortunately, there is no danger, so long as I say
nothing.

HEDDA

Are you trying to control a human destiny,
Judge?

BRACK

Dearest Hedda—believe me—I will not abuse my
power.

HEDDA

No you won't.

*Hedda walks to the bookcase, back turned to
the others, takes the pistol out of the case.*

BRACK

People generally get used to the inevitable.

HEDDA

How are you getting on, George?

GEORGE

It will be months of work.

HEDDA

Back still turned away

Doesn't it seem strange to you, Thea? You sitting
with George—just as you used to sit with Eric?

THEA

Ah, if I could only inspire your husband in the
same way!

HEDDA
Is there nothing I can do to help you two?

GEORGE
No, nothing in the world. I trust you will keep
Hedda company while we work, Judge.

BRACK
With the greatest of pleasure.

HEDDA
I see.

> *Without looking at any of them, Hedda exits*
> *through the glass door.*

GEORGE
This work is distressing her. I'll tell you what,
Thea—you take the empty room at Aunt Julia's,
and then I'll come over in the evenings, and we
can work there.

> *A shot is heard. George, Thea, and Brack*
> *leap to their feet.*

GEORGE
She is playing with those pistols again.

BRACK
People don't do such things.

> *Blackout.*

THE END

About Stephen Evans

Stephen Evans is a playwright and the author of *The Island of Always, Whose Beauty is Past Change,* and *Funny Thing Is: A Guide to Understanding Comedy.*

Find him online at:

https://www.istephenevans.com/

STEPHEN EVANS

Books by Stephen Evans

Plays:

The Visitation Quartet:
  The Ghost Writer
  Monuments
  Tourists
  Spooky Action at a Distance
  At the Still Point

Experience	*Three plays about Ralph Waldo Emerson*
Generations	*(with Morey Norkin and Michael Gilles)*
As You Like It	*(by William Shakespeare, adapted by Stephen Evans)*
The Glass Door	*(An adaptation of Hedda Gabler by Henrik Ibsen)*

Non-Fiction:

Funny Thing Is: A Guide to Understanding Comedy
Anthropomorphosis
Small Gifts
Liebestraum
The Laughing String: Thoughts on Writing

Fiction:

The Marriage of True Minds
The Island of Always:
The Marriage Gift
Whose Beauty is Past Change
The Mind of a Writer and other Fables
Memory Plays
Epigrammaticon
The Next Joy and the Next

Verse:

Limerosity
Limerositus
Sonets from the Chesapeke
The Crooked Mirror

STEPHEN EVANS

www.ingramcontent.com/pod-product-compliance
Lightning Source LLC
Chambersburg PA
CBHW021651120626
46545CB00002B/807